Contradictions

for Richard Calarco

"But, as you see, here I am, after ordeals suffered
And twenty years of journeying, come home to my native land.
This transformation was worked by Athena, the Commander,
Who has the power to make of me what she chooses—
Sometimes a beggar; sometimes a man with youthful body finely clothed.
It is easy for the sovereign gods in spacious heaven
Both to elevate a man and, again, to knock him down."

—*The Odyssey*, XVI, author's translation

Contents

Contradictions

The Common Thread

In the graphic textiles of experience,
Where themes are threads, trace the one that runs,
First, through the fable of the compliant Cat
Who combed red coals (the Monkey goading, scolding)
To rake out toasted chestnuts tittering guile
Could then with unharmed fingers peel and eat,
Not *one* left for the dupe who scorched her paw;
That, and the clemency of Coriolanus,
Sparing ancestral Rome a bloody sack,
His banishment, meanwhile, still not rescinded;
And the French maxim noting that we all
Have fortitude enough to endure the torment
Of persons not ourselves; or gibes lobbed at
The man forsaken: "Others he saved, himself
He cannot save."
                        Like common thread, serene
Expedience outstrips the speed of insight,
Consolidating patches of a quilt
To keep complacency snug as toast—for instance,
The donors who, instead of food or shelter,
Sent cast-off, threadbare T-shirts to survivors
Of the hurricane, a few with printed slogans,
Home truths like, "Life's a bitch, and then you die."

Memory

Black pentacles, abrupt shadows in flight
wheel across ranks of brick, high, windowed walls
at the end of backyard gardens opposite.
Silence, ground note of the late and early year,
climbs from floor level to a half-light fallen
among red peppers, garlic, Winesap apples.
In the desk drawer, a sacheted cache of letters
stamped with flags, with heroes, birds or flowers.

States, whole climates and terrains from here
(a chill to count how many years it's been),
she'd take up thread or scissors and begin
sewing together printed panels, each window in turn
provided—or appeased—with curtains. Curtains
opened to let day in, or closed against the night.

Intervals

A quick, shy glance shot toward the window
As the person behind you leaves the room
(Floors bare, a complex fretwork oak parquet)

So that you hear a volley of steps, exeunts
Knocking along what has to be the hallway.

Between each heel-tap and the next falls
A starry, human silence—

Brief, and always the same duration,
Even though if your eyes followed
The silhouette
Would grow smaller the farther

It retreated down the hall.

Intervals regular as notches on a clock face,
And yet that short-term excerpt
Between footfalls spans

"Colossal" distances, whole eras in epitome
At volumes waiting to be amplified:

Drop after underground drop of liquid limestone,
Wobbling bleats in lowland pastures, a thermal
Gust that fans out long blades of the hawk's wing,

Cyclone of a drill biting into concrete,
Echoed reports as a cliff of ice cracks,
Shears off a glacier and plunges
To the crinkling, blue-black, polar sea.

If the sound of those steps stopped short,

You couldn't resist turning around
To reconnoiter the dim hall, each flanking
Door resonant as the sound box of a cello.

"Are you there?" No answer means you'll pause
For a while, staring down the undeniable;
And, when you turn back into the room,

Hear your own steps, each distanced
From its successor by a vigilant
Silence that might (or not?) be broken
By the muted hammer-stroke

Of another footfall. As long as it is
Not, that elastic interval will serve
As conduit for audible signals, syllables,
Thumps, buzzes, whispers, clangs from elsewhere—

Glacier, drill, wing-blade, sheep;

The bearded St. Petersburg cantor sobbing his antiphon;
A heron splashing down in the Everglades.

Who, What, Where, When, Why?

Rumor, the homemade metamorphosis;
That with each telling modifies its key
Adjectives, its semicolons; that scales
The afternoon, beyond the towers' nth floor,
A geyser of invention, a carnival
Lingo disseminated on winds of envy,
Calculation, itch for the fecund dirt.

No kangaroo court so summary as rumor,
Dispensing with the drab credential-check,
Skirting obstructive rules of evidence,
Always with an eye to the camera,
Always lobbying for conviction, however
Listless the testimony, however queasy.

Those times when prosecution aced its game?
A human metaphor stood for sentencing,
The lifelong upshot sealed in lead, since rumor
Makes no provisions for parole—or any
Amendment that might heal a broken statute.
Defendant reads a lot, no? Most of you do.
Some find the Stoic writings helpful. Try them.

The Bandwagon

A tiny speck on the horizon.

Which doesn't move or doesn't seem to yet
Must be on the move; has enlarged, is now

The size of a thumb, and now still larger, look,
A newly gilded vehicle rocking and racketing
Down the pike. Beyond the band—uniformed,

Gold-braided, their coiled brasses aglitter—
A few grand figureheads clutch a post,
They wave and fire off grins at onlookers, who,
The eagerest, respond by lunging for a ladder

Dangled from the wagon, climb and are dragged
Onto the flatbed by earlier troops, welcomed
As opportune endorsements of their program,
Another, another, and another! And some
Impressive knot of adherents they are,

Arms on shoulders, the victor's strut,
A promo for dazzled joiners farther on,
Who scuttle and jump to swell their ranks.
Each wheel turns faster, revving up
For the straightaway, hickory spokes
A blur like an electric fan at top speed,

Scribbles of gleam smeared across it.
Faster, closer, numbers snowballing
According to an exponent that also mounts.
Yet, nothing daunted, they swing aboard, dying
To be the in-crowd, the A-list, the blue-chips.
Hup! It's party time, tap this keg and chug
Your suds, we won-won-won, and we're one

High roller of a club, hotshots all, bigger, louder,
United stumpers we stand, sterling but humble.
Course now, we feel sorry for you sadsacks
Out there who fumbled the ball, who didn't latch on
Quick enough. But hang cool, we'll give you a boost
When we get a chance, why, sure. Meantime, ha ha,
Eat our dust! And then—then, like a flashbulb, it's gone.
Sudden stillness. Still here... In open space, morning sun.

Which toplights the trees and their strange, shining leaves.

Double Portrait with Refrigerator Magnets

Which never held in place a house and yard
crayoned by kids we didn't have or adopt
(chimney leaking a tangled yarn of smoke,
garden path flanked with daffs or daisies). No,
just a list of chores and who performed them last
beside a creased snapshot of Chris and me
arm in arm on the apartment balcony.

One dime-size lodestone glued to a multi-towered
strip of Manhattan skyline, with the caption,
"New York, New York! Come Be a Part of It."
No one had to tell me my tall intended
from Ohio viewed a Gotham City condo
as an extra perk. He said "I do" to this
unmonolithic piece of the rock as well.

Hop inside our tomthumb replica
of a panel truck, banner headline posted
on the driver side plugging Effective Plumbing—
24 Hour Service—to be specific,
Drains Cleaned Hot Water Heaters Renovations.
Just telephone this number, printed red
on the door: 545-0110.

In low relief, a plastic souvenir
bought in our nation's capital at a stand
near 1600 Pennsylvania Ave.
The White House. All right, it was a joke.
How else get serious about abstractions
like *freedom* and *the pursuit of happiness*?
But no one's hoisted the rainbow flag there yet.

We had for a year or so a Christmas angel
in white and gilded robe, clasping some sheet
music—"Peace on earth, good will," and so forth.
The singer fell and broke a wing, but straggled
back home. Then fell again and lost the spare.
A final plunge left gilt crumbs everywhere,
the magnet proven not quite strong enough.

More stable's been the still from *I Love Lucy*
(reruns of which Chris sometimes likes to watch).
The foursquare metal excerpt sticks like gum;
which means we can henceforth expect to see
Mrs. Arnaz wince down a bitter spoonful
of patent medicine that she's been hired
to pitch to folks on the other side of TV.

The little magnet once too weak to float our angel
has been recycled and seems able to (so far)
support that picture, two euphoric newlyweds
smiling into the future—as, given what they knew,
they were fully entitled to do... Meanwhile, these lines,
scrawled in crayon, can hang beside them, held in place
by a stolid blue-and-white-striped giveaway
thanking the clients of Manhattan Mini-Storage.

Asynchronic

I'd been doing that, going out just after sunset—
the sky a bowl of blue-green light,
a basin filled with cold, still seawater.

Shops in the advancing dusk looked like fish tanks
flooded with neutral overhead lighting that fell
on personnel about to close up for the day.
When I tugged back a sleeve, the wrist was naked—
forgot my watch again—and both hands chapped and rough.
Why do our hands have five fingers, no more, and no less?
Zoologists would know. Meanwhile
one of the routine, strictly business
clocks glimpsed through windows
during the rounds of my unofficial beat
could substitute for a watch. The first said 6:25;
the second, several storefronts down, 6:22;
a third, 6:29. Time didn't agree with itself.
Tonight, it didn't agree with me, either;
but then it never entirely had (and never will?).

A white-haired man with olive skin and tattered clothes
limped into Met Food and panhandled the clerk,
one I recognized, her face mild and familiar as bread.
For half a second—strange—it felt permanent,
indestructible as the tiny gleam
that pearled in the dark pupil of her eye.
6:33... And now a go-getter poised at 6:45.

Evening star in a sky by then blue-black ink,
and I roughly fifteen minutes older,
arms dangling at my sides.
But no wiser, only a bit farther
into the walk, with a sudden hunger pang,
the gut's alarm bell, sounding dinner hour.

All I'd seen, the streets, the clock faces,
menagerie of the populous city, were saying
(so to speak), "Feast your eyes on this."
If the banquet had agreed with me,
and if I'd had a shelter to return to...
Time had moved in back there, a silent
dimension unconcerned that it would turn us
out on the street (first you, and after
you'd gone, then me), according to some
ironclad schedule followed or policed
at glacial speed by supervising hands...
Or, worse, when my door swung open,
by spidery digitals that glared
across the darkened room with their 6:58—

numbers reflected counter, greener, flamelike
(detail, the lost-and-found of deity)
in the crystal of the watch I left there on the table.

My Last June in Chelsea

Men in tank tops strolled or marched up Eighth,
dozens in their deep tans, too many to count,
a male shyness disguised as "attitude."
Beside us, traffic shot the rapids, brakes slamming,
headlights coming on as the day's-end afterglow dimmed.

The indolence, the redolence of attraction,
its riddle: Why him and not him? Ironic innocence,
a smooth, loose-hung construction easy in his stride,
sizing up passing mirrors returning the compliment.
I saw and wasn't seen; almost, but didn't quite belong.

*

New York continues as itself by changing,
Chelsea the latest of its Cinderella
makeovers. Who'd have guessed, that move-in day,
I'd keep its zip code longer than any other

since the primeval streets and gardens of home?
Fifteen years back this neighborhood was pegged
as the Village's sleepy upper story, an attic
jumbled with memories, seminarians,

"A Visit from St. Nicholas," a low-rent
barrio where some stellar artists lived.
My mentor David, too, the smiling host
of savvy parties on 22nd Street—

until his death in the mid-'80s, decade
of megabucks and memorial services.
One day I counted; but stopped at thirty-three.
How many dead survive survivor's guilt?

*

End of the years with one, start of the years
with a second (in coyspeak) "significant other."
What was all that optimism based on?
Two apartments, two breakups: It happened here.

*

A man I used to notice on Ninth in the teens: Latino,
not young, with the birth condition of short legs, who hung
outside a deli there, its odd-job caretaker.
Battleship gray, face deeply lined, he still looked strong,
busy, deferred to by his unemployed compañeros.

Weekday mornings you would stride along and pass them
all on your daily hike to work. Ever wonder
what it would be like to live his life? I did.
To some he might have seemed commendable, a hero;
stoic, and not, so far as one could tell, embittered.

Just once our eyes met; and knew, however briefly
long the moment lasted, who returned the gaze,
some sort of shoot-from-the-hip telepathy… Strange
how rage at my own shortcomings cooled in that exchange
with the hindered (but resourceful) soul-man of the place.

*

Evening of the Pride Parade. The fireworks' volcanic
stained glass viewed from my terrace by wowed or blasé friends.
Last shooting stars burnt out, I glanced down at the street,
where two men, deep in discussion, leaned against a wall—
not the same age, both, in different ways, appealing.

One final clinch before they stepped apart. One final
serious look; and then they turned and walked outside
the viewfinder… I guess you had to be there… Or maybe
not, and farther on, some other place or person
would also "signify." But… that was my last June in Chelsea.

And Then I Saw

My body, laid out on a marble slab.
Naked but for a linen sheet tucked under
Its chin, as though to keep the patient warm.

A solemn band approached; identified
The late departed with what looked like mingled
Relief, mild satisfaction, and bereavement.

One of them took away an arm—the right,
Was it?—and loped off with a spring in his step.
Which prompted others to do likewise: here

A shoulder (suitable for crying on),
there a foot, there an eye and there an ear.
Plump already, one scooped out the belly.

Just who you'd imagine claimed the head.
Not the one I hoped tugged loose a rib.
Some, by no means all, I knew as friends;

But felt no bitterness, instead, acceptance.
This, while watching their several withdrawals,
Travelers moving farther out and deeper

Into the ringing distance—who all began
To flourish, somehow more intently themselves
Than they had earlier resolved to be.

Was glad of that, despite a fit of shivers
(Simple human nature still presiding)
When I took note of the rummage that remained,

Wishing a greener plot had been marked out
For what had breathed with so much spark and promise.
My turn, then, to come forward for a closer

Look; and, since no one else had carried off
That steady, flexibly strung pump at rest
Beneath the sternum, take it for my own,

Sensing its mute but anchored trust that parts
Lucky for others would befriend as well—
Oh love—even the heir that flesh once named.

The Mousetrap

for Nikolas Stangos and David Plante

'Tis the day after Christmas, London, Boxing Day, twelve noon,
A.D. 2000. Outdoors,
as *Hamlet*'s sentry (Act I, Scene i) says, "Not a mouse stirring."

On Baker Street, though, once you stir, you'll spy, through parted curtains,
a matron dressed in blue,
boxing up surplus presents to be sent on to the needy.

(Thoughtful friends proposed and underwrote my holiday,
three weeks in Marylebone…
So, church mouse, rack your brains, and find a way of conveying thanks.)

No special rep for largesse stars the name of Arthur C. Doyle,
whose alter ego lodged
here at 221B, now "The Sherlock Holmes Museum."

Trinkets in its shop window dangle from a dozen hooks.
And the cleaner's farther down
sports this notice, save the mark, in gold: WE WILL DYE FOR YOU.

Today's also the Feast of Stephen. They wrapped *him* up, all right,
with punches to the gut,
left jabs of stone, and, match done, sepulchre carved out of same.

(A boxed red set of martyrdom the *Golden Legend* gave
the poor—stonemasons, some
of them, and bricklayers, whose patron pious black humor named him.)

Underground's the quickest transport to my matinee,
Agatha Christie's *Tourist
Trap*, I mean, *The Mousetrap*, Guinness record for long runs.

St. Martin's Theatre is crammed, cramped, dowdy; in its creaky
way stately, with
the columns and dark panels of a country house in Kent.

Curtain up on blackness: screams, a scuffle. Follows a none
too bright comedy
of murders enlivening a B&B named Monkswell Manor.

Christie's gambits resemble that old board game *Clue*: "Colonel Mustard
did it; in the Den;
with the Knife," we'd guess and keep on guessing till we solved the case.

The play's canonic theme song, "Three Blind Mice," has its own perp,
an unnamed farmer's wife,
who cut off their tails, et cetera, before they "bought the farm."

Don't try to grasp a Mother Goose rhyme, and even less our pomo
poetry or Ophelia's
word-salads, which consumers "botch up fit to their own thoughts."

The Prince of Denmark's play within the play's the same sly thing,
a detective Rorschach set
to catch the conscience of the king... and titled *The Mouse-trap*.

Coincidence. The minute it strikes, take cover, private eye!
Christie's got designs
on you. If conscience is the game, though, how does she figure it?

As a purblind mouse, I guess, whose twitching nose sniffs something rotten
and ferrets out repressed
mischief—each playgoer, A.C. suggests, a Mickey Rex.

*

Curtain, bows. An actor moments earlier nailed as culprit
steps forward and makes us
flattered accessories pledge not to give away the ending.

(Bait that initiates would dangle, keeping the box office
busy for almost half
a century, the die-hard run itself an extra hype.)

Meanwhile, the author's books have sold, worldwide, a *billion* copies.
Why do we so love murder?
A mystery (like the Incarnation) that still remains unsolved.

My guess: "Detective fiction's our response to the withdrawing
tide of faith, when God,
if not Old Nick, was snuffed by evolution, astrophysics.

To prove no gates of Hades yawned, our inner centurion
stalked the Place of the Skull
and whipped out tools. In the lab, with science, clues suggest, *we* done it.

And then felt guilty..." Plausible? Even applaudable.
But, as I step outside
and slog through mist and dark, more dialogue: *So typical.*

Always boxing yourself in with abstract speculation,
poor substitute for feeling
your concrete circumstances. True, but it helps protect me. *From?*

Peanut gallery catcalls like, "Jeez, will someone please toss
a dropcloth over his cage."
Emulate princeling spleen re blacklisting, skulduggery?

No thanks. Abstraction springs the lock and helps us build (archaic
smile in place) a verbal
construct—thank you, Stevens—lighter, limberer than stone.

*

Home to New York again. The months tick by to strike late March,
today's park ramble ending
at the Cloisters' gate. I'll see a Gothic amulet starred with diamonds;

a pear tree's angular espalier fixed to weathered limestone;
the Unicorn in his paddock.
For only a Virgin could detain him—one like that ingenue

there in Campin's *Annunciation.* The facts: Saint Gabriel did it
with a breathing ray of light
in the betrothed's neat inglenook, she reading a book of hours.

Flanked, too, by other clues: a candle just then snuffed; a polished
ewer; a lily Ophelia
never caroled. Fact, symbol, fused in oil paint fluent as chrism.

Left-panel donors, keen first-nighters in rich trappings, queue up.
In the right, Saint Joseph's shop,
where he sits drilling, planing, nailing, top-hinged wooden shutters

hooked open inward to admit a Flemish view of Nazareth. Bend
closer. On the sill,
contraption for sale: a mousetrap, cocked for action. Ah. He'd read

Augustine: "The Cross of the Anointed was the Demon's mousetrap."
Build the best prototype,
and the world will beat a path to your door. Then clemency pleas can be

lodged with the carpenter's wife, I guess? From felicity abstracted,
the saeculum's long run
designed—alas, poor Yorick—to make a case for each wounded name.

Jerusalem

Then keep thy heart....
Melville, *Clarel*

They will lift up their heads:
the Lion Gate, St. Stephen's, the New,
Jaffa, and, last, the Gate of Dung.
The gates will lift up their heads
that the King of Glory may come in.

As Judah means "Praised," its chief city will be
more highly praised, the ramparts and towers
of David's citadel praised and exalted.

*

Come this far, how close the door on what
not even they had stubbornness enough to bar?
The Rock where Isaac, his wrists bound tight,
saw above him a face clench in agony
moments before an angel dove down to stay
Abraham's hand is now perpetual,
preserved in the furnace of tradition
along with that ram whose horn became the shofar.

—Or is it rock as fact, one of the sights,
coated with dust and roofed with a golden dome
reverberant with a murmured sura
expanding on the Prophet's airborne nocturnal
journey, which fixed him like a star
on the cusp of the crescent moon?

*

Just as the present-day pilgrim goes from station
to station in a loud array of discount tours,
tenants have reconstrued the basilica
of the Holy Sepulchre as real estate
for hereditary zeal to balkanize
among several sects. Each has its sharply
defended square yardage of theology, but none
equals that stone niche off to one side where an oil lamp's
starred wick baffles the sway of archaic shadows.

*

The Temple abides in its myth
but also in limestone fact, at least the part
Roman demolition experts failed
to pound into undatable rubble.
Foundation Wall, you won't be alone again,
alive with the Shekhinah's quiet thunder,
bloodwarm dovecote of fissured building blocks
into which ten thousand handwritten
praises or lamentations have flown.

*

And Via Dolorosa toils south from Gabbatha's
courtyard, where a few detached centurions
gave their charge the prescribed flogging
before sending him on his forced march.
A path useless to retrace without spiriting away
two millennia or any obstacle
to contemplation of punished flesh at ground zero
staggering forward under a massive wooden T,
palm fronds still underfoot, but dry and broken,
whispering hosannas no one hears.

Because a Procurator exercised available
options, the name "Pilate" survives globally
on the lips of millions when the Credo's recited
tenets descend into history and make it faith.

*

What was truth? What will it be?
For the condemned whose breath comes shorter and shorter,
"Even death may prove unreal at the last"—unreal,
like the sound of a tree fallen to earth
far from any ear, or any human ear.
When the body atoned to its trunk and limbs toppled
out of time, did it finally become audible
to his listeners? To some. To Clarel, and for later
pilgrims who risked as much as one step beyond doubt.

No other dispatch could outdistance the silence
following on that farewell to his friend—
who, standing at the Place of the Skull,
heard him say, "Woman, behold thy son,"
as prelude to, "Behold thy mother."
Seeing where sons of earth were bound to go,
from that day forth he housed a second mother under his roof.

Lift up your heads.

The Author of Torah

The blessing safely lifted onto Joshua's shoulders,
Moses climbed up Mount Nebo, high above Moab.
Tendons winced as he bent to retie a sandal, and haze
flooded his vision, which had nothing to see
(or black rock and scrub thorn only) until he stopped
and said, I will wait here for the voice of the Most High.

You showed him all the land—
Gilead, the hills of Ephraim and Manasseh,
from Judah to the western sea as far as Zoar.
And said: Your eyes have seen what I promised,
yet, because at Meribah-Kadesh
you failed to manifest the holiness I am,
you do not go in.

At that distance and from the heights
Moses stood and watched as the children
of Israel began the westward trek.
His sight strengthened and he saw each one.
The mother, thin and staring, bent down
to take her firstborn's hand,
who cried and then laughed.
The young brothers with new beards
and faces blackened by years in Sinai, strode along
carrying all they had rolled up in a sheepskin.
The white-haired elder and his mourning wife,
whose only daughter was lost in the desert,
stalked slowly forward without speaking.
An orphaned girl, her cousin, and her cousin's husband
discussed it quietly and held hands.
A concert of voices, murmurs, cries, laughter,
rising, falling, babbling like water,
the fountain of Meribah-Kadesh that sprang
from a wall of rock in the desert
when Moses struck it with his staff.

Days of his life returned to him.
One last time he saw Miriam's serious gaze
during the hours of instruction. He recalled
the harp players in Pharaoh's summer palace;
white noonday and the shadow of his hand
raised to strike the Egyptian overseer;
Zipporah's fear and trust when Jethro urged her forward;
the brush-tree that spoke out in tongues of fire;
Egypt's plagues; blood on the doorposts for a sign;
the exiles' safe conduct across marshlands
among bulrushes as seabirds called overhead;
mutiny and lightning in the desert;
a pillar of smoke by day, and fire by night.

The moment drew near as those he was
bound to and had contended with went up
to a land of hills dusted with the first spring green.
Sheep stopped their grazing to stare; like an intake
of breath, a lull suspended the low hum
hovering around hillsides in flower.
His eyes filled with tears. And silver bands of sun
broke from a veil of cloud overhead
down to the plain of Moab, lighting the face
of Joshua on one side, so that half
remained in shadow.

At that moment Moses was taken to his people.
His body is said to be buried at Beth-Peor, yet
the grave has never been found.

The grave has never been found—
and Joshua led the Israelites westward into Canaan.

After Celan

Suns made of thread
above a waste land of ash and soot.
A tree-
high insight
holds the note the light strikes: there
are still texts to sing beyond
the confines of the human.

Dawn of Evening

The windows earlier molten gold
Are ductile timpani now, cooled
In solutions of a milder light
That rinse the view with second sight.

Which hour salves as many pains?
Little that twilight veils is real.
Time's inverse periodic remains
To see your mettle tempered steel.

Tenebrae

Blind items, bits you scan in gossip columns:
"What Wall Street CEO was seen with what
berhinestoned starlet late last night at CALLAS,
one of the posher downtown watering holes?"
Or *blind ambition,* stepping on the gas,
hindered or helped by concurrent blind ambition.
Or *blind alley,* into which the stroller
turns—a site where freedom doesn't ring.
Or *love's blindfold,* its darkling precondition...
and *blind faith,* that pilots by dead reckoning.

*

It seemed at first a minor irritation.
Readers all get them, "floaters," see-through jellies
or what look like microorganisms
enlarged a thousand X, an infiltration
of fog that creeps across the empty page.
Freak product of myopia and fatigue,
they vanish when we give our eyes a rest
(or when some passage makes us prey to nothing
more invasive than the printed word).

This one felt eerier, though maybe just
a travel jitter, symptom of a first
visit to Germany? Whatever the cause,
here swam a minnow in the drink of vision,
its aquarium the vitreous humor
of my eye (during that week occupied
transmitting form and color, painting, sculpture
from the world over gathered in Berlin—
works found there only, not some happier place).

A gauzelike ghostling drifted through each one,
Saint Lucy with her tray of fresh-peeled glimmers,
Oedipus pleading with the oracle,
or—antiquity's leanest, highest paid
top model—Nefertiti, whose New Kingdom
crown was an upward flaring, Nile-blue conic
section, and royal necklace a rayed sunburst
like the human iris (her own right pupil black
with the imbibed night of three millennia).

The left eye gone, an alabaster socket
able, I guess, to plumb the Realm of Shadows,
but useless at ground zero. Incinerated,
was it, by staring at the sun-disk Aton
(whom her own sibling spouse proclaimed sole god)
to detonate an even greater depth charge
than the third D, horizons in recession
gauged henceforth if at all by sifting sand
that buried, then withdrew from Ikhetaten...

Her long-stemmed neck, head forward in a graceful
slump, ichthyomorphic eyeliner and sungold
skin, her evident pride in having lived
for art and love, composed an icon willing
to countenance, in apparent calm, erasure
of the Memphian gods and all their monuments,
horn and beak toppled from a thousand thrones,
engulfed in worship of the One, whose dawn
trained on her body the infrared of truth.

*

Berlin-to-Dresden transit via train
put time (a shorter stretch of it) on rewind
again, the present town—part old and part
period renovation—supplanted by
a frozen night from 1945,

30

when cones of spotlight from low-flown warplanes
targeted sites below, the domes and spires
of Saxony's own Florence, *Stadt der Kunst,*
the Brühlsche Terrasse an outdoors console
where pastel figurines in porcelain

gathered and strolled, filigree passages
from Zelenka or Winckelmann afloat
in the background of consciousness—until
incendiary gods ex machina
unleashed their high-tech eschaton, which flamed

in the black steel mirror of the Elbe
as Zwinger Palace and Semper Oper bowed
to the volcano, extra emphasis
pumped into a clear-cut Allied message
addressed in fiery terms to the Führer.

*

Postmodern odysseys conclude with jet lag.
My door swung open on a tiled foyer
recalled verbatim but grown unfamiliar—
the wraithlike floater (oh no) a new component
in long establishing shots that picked their way

over sofa, lamp, framed drawing, open book.
And if a gaunt six-leggèd tenant winnowed
tiny antennae in hopes at last of dinner,
and if I chased him with a dirty look
and muttered threats like *Muori dannato! Muori!,*

was the operatic tantrum partly fueled
by unacknowledged fear, now that home
(the fabled castle) had as well become
nest for a visual parasite? It must
have been, otherwise why would I have scheduled

the very next day a visit with my eye
doctor? Who dosed both pupils with whatever
has replaced belladonna and in his dry
appraiser's voice described a retinal tear,
lymphatic leakage in the vitreous humor,

retina risking complete detachment. (A risk,
in psychologic terms, I'd courted before,
never dreaming it might turn literal.)
The gemlike beam that plays a CD disc,
believe it or not, would perform the task

of atonement—A Minor Operation
only a rotten coward couldn't manage.
So let the Laser Symphony begin,
machine-gunned flashbulbs in collaboration
play magic fire, scored on a living page

with dissonant synesthesia, piercing hues,
gold-green, red-violet, the retina veined
like an ivy leaf with vessels darkly stained
or thorn branches against a sky all bruise
where each crescendo flared, till none remained.

*

A week without reading. Boredom, creeping illiteracy.
Solace of music and the word at least sung—
Tosca, Die ägyptische Helena. Fiftieth
anniversary of V-E Day on TV, eyesight
improving, and then—I don't believe it—
The Return of the Floater.

So, at the follow-up with Dr. Ransome,
who pronounced our retina nicely on the mend,
I asked him when this—*slime* I saw would go.

With a humor not exactly brittle but, say,
vitreous, he laughed, "Oh no, we didn't zap
the little floater. It stays. It's your friend
for life." I saw. (And see.) With friends like that—.

*

Still, no complaints from someone spared the fate
of all those one-eyed jacks in Egyptian friezes.
Patience, lower the blinds, and let repairs
firm up. The leak's been plugged. Meanwhile, I am
able again to read and recognize
a daylit world in depth and odd detail;
also, the world of art—good reproductions
of which were all I brought home from Berlin.

Right now, in fact, an unframed Nefertiti
is propped next to the PC screen. And if
this once the words lined up there voice her mute
appeal, while poetry, faith's younger sibling,
provides safe conduct to a mythos still
operative at least in song—no matter;
the aria doubles as an exit visa
back to a future nothing stopped from dawning:

Aton, O invincible eye of day,
Repair the charred arena of our vision,
Eclipse of war's destructions send away.
Now let old insight speak with new precision
And learn from unknowing clouds what not to say.

Long-Distance Call to a Friend Who Lived with AIDS As Long As He Could

Because we hooked up most days courtesy
of Ma Bell, only now and then arranging
to meet for lunch or coffee, it's your graveled,
ambling voice I miss, the live connection
"no longer in service," as the sound bite says.

Remember that haiku I jotted down
on a café napkin several years back?
How cities, even with their gridlock, noise,
and pollution, also sheltered gardens? Your eyes
crinkled with pleasure: Those cool, green, inward places—.

The one you've moved to may not yet be wired
for cellular, but here's my morning call,
dialed by habit or a "burning desire"
to speak. And how much does it matter if
the message and the channel are the same?

Though Asian verseforms seldom clicked for me,
they hung the moon for you, so here's a haiku
six-pack for the picnic, sent in hopes
of getting a smile again. At least on my side
any image would that brought you back.

*

Red oak leaves floating
On clear water and, below,
Speckled rainbow trout.

*

Stripped by cold or blight,
Bare elm trees. On a high branch,
Clumps of mistletoe.

*

March snow falls and falls.
Droplets bead down my window.
Cloud, light, one substance.

*

A single reindeer
Moves north across the frost-white tundra.
Fog. The rising sun.

*

Spring winds. Mourning dove,
Perched on the telephone line,
Is it warm up there?

*

July Fourth. Blue eyes,
Glancing up from a full plate,
Smile so hard they close.

"The Report of My Death Was an Exaggeration"

Mark Twain, in a note to the London Office of The New York Herald

Think of it as a fault-line fantasy
that gets dressed up in mauve and black
and latches on to certain people—
figures who excite debate, at least.

Mark had popularity going for him.
He wrote like a champ and was a nice guy
off the court as well. From him you'd always
get an aerial view of the subject,
whatever subject, and end up knowing
more than you had before liftoff.

He'd fling open a door to the neat four-room
tree-house of his heart and let you in,
despite palpable risk to circulation,
not to mention loss of privacy.

Still, it moved, and the obit that everyone
expected to be reading any day now
kept on not appearing, it just wouldn't.

It wouldn't, and, though people are eager to hear
the sequel, sorry, not Mark, but instead this *topic*
's been terminated—no, seriously, I mean it.

A Window on the Strait of Juan de Fuca

for Sam Hamill

You should be here now, Sam, watching your poems—
the way they dart, swoop, swerve, and glide; or startle
up in flexible constellations; perch
in tandem on humming power lines; or work
in teams to comb the grass for grubs or seeds.

Last night's cold front countersigned the dark,
unwinding one of your strongest as it sheared
miles-long bolts of silk against the eaves,
some tattered scroll with an account, in ink-brush,
of a long trek through cloudflown mountain peaks and forests;
and then, at dusk, skies clear and windless, the eased,
upward-looming arc of Kannon at the full.

This noon, short lyrics flank the paths,
dapper, as the air stirs them,
in azure, rosé, egg-yolk, damson, white—
radial symmetry or simple furls,
a simplicity not at all ruffled
by Latin names lent them by Linnaeus.

Your summation, Sam? It rests in broad marine expanses
framed by the headland spruces' spiky silhouette,
an elemental blue that paler sea-lanes river
in concurrence with surveying rafts of cloud.
Wave after wave keeps reconfiguring the grain,
waters invariant by virtue of constant flux—
all the more at daybreak when a further
laminate of diamond breaks the surface of
the page's rising tide, light infinitely *not there:*
and hence perpetual from now forward.

A Walrus Tusk from Alaska

Arp might have done a version in white marble,
the model held aloft, in approximate awe:
this tough cross-section oval of tusk,
dense and cool as fossil cranium—

preliminary bloodshed condonable
if Inupiat hunters on King Island may
follow as their fathers did the bark of a husky,
echoes ricocheted from roughed-up eskers

on the glacier, a resonance salt-cured
and stained deep green by Arctic seas, whose tilting floor
mirrors the mainland's snowcapped amphitheater.
Which of his elders set Mike Saclamana the task

and taught him to decide, in scrimshaw, what was so?
Netted incisions black as an etching
saw a way to scratch in living infinitives
known since the Miocene to have animated

the Bering Strait: one humpback whale, plump,
and bardic; an orca caught on the ascending arc,
salt droplets flung from a flange of soot-black fin...
Farther along the bone conveyor belt a small

ringed seal will never not be swimming, part-time
landlubber, who may feel overshadowed by the donor
walrus ahead. And by his scribal tusk, which stands
in direct correspondence to the draftsman's burin,

skillful enough to score their tapeloop ostinato,
no harp sonata, but, instead, the humpback whale's
yearning bassoon (still audible if you cup
the keepsake to your ear and let it sound the depths).

Photography

Who would deal events an instant silence,
rethinking them in black and white and gray?
The eye that says, "Hold still," while awe exempts
[one smaller, straight-edged quadrant of a site]
from the mudslide attrition of day-by-day.

A click's enough to frame a face, a body
[the psyche coaxed outside to show herself],
pausing for a breath that, living still,
vision inhales each time I identify—
or do so with—her mime in monochrome.

*

Photographer, gleaner of epiphanies:

Sepia angle of a Pyramid
egypting the nineteenth-century background,
[one camel's heavy-lidded trance under sawtooth palms].

*

On the propylaeum steps, beneath a scarred Ionic column,
[two stoic guides, crouched, hugging their knees]
sit tight for the exposure and the duration.

*

[A phaeton stopping at the Place de l'Opéra.]
[Crowds surging across the London Bridge.]

*

[Niagara's marble avalanche.]
[Apache chief, wincing at the flash.]
[Confederate grays, bearded troops now dead in perpetuity.]
[Locomotive charting a westward course under frozen coal-smoke.]
[Yosemite and its surveyor.]

                    *

[Line without end,
immigration at Ellis Island],
applicants whose first lives have reached
a terminal, praying the papers for resurrection
won't be rubber-stamped DENIED.

                    *

Then from our own wrecked century, reportage
feeding the magazines to make them lifelike:
[Depression.] [Popular Front.] [A dictator in midair.]
Documents heaped up, stacked like cords of wood,
like the dead, [charnel that just missed incineration],
dispersion in silver billows of anonymity...
[The bomb.] [Famine.] [Nightstick marrying a temple.]

                    *

And all across the latter decades, backyards native
to Atlanta and Portland, Topeka and Eureka, feature
[Mom in Bermudas, Dad at the grill, kids with their fads].
[The wedding], [the christening], restaged after the event—
one, two, three, snap!—in a more perfect perfection.
Sweet album, be it ever so humble, there's no place like.

                    *

Photographer, record yourself in a time-lapse shot:

[Your body backed by the Pyramids.]
[Your face smiling from the Acropolis.]
[You, a stroller on the London Bridge.]
[You, silhouetted against the white noise of Niagara.]
[You and yours on the ferry to Ellis Island.]

*

Each negative went down into baptismal darkrooms,
first nocturnity rinsed away to resurface in white
and fine-grained shades of blackened silver. All that tech
can save, arcades, statues, rainforests, icebergs, skylines,
movie stills, road signs, what we have been, what lived,
trivial or grand: our treasure and out of reach, springs
long gone, whose available sun will never set.

AMERICAN PORTRAITS

1. Bloodwork

Somebody's got to do it, even if you
could *define* ho-hum by this job, each sample
analyzed one by one, and best not cheat,
because, though most of them check clean, a few
come from people with a major problem.

Serum tells the truth to those with training—
training she busted it to get, five-figure
school loans and overdrawn accounts of nerve.
Still, Pops was the one who cried at graduation:
"I always hoped you'd have the things I didn't..."

At least *her* blood is healthy, with one eighth
African, one half Choctaw, and the balance,
white. (Genetic math.) But, shoot, in this country,
one drop of black blood means that you are black,
so just relax and do your work. Next sample:

Red cells and white, and then invisible
viruses to transform the ambient,
seasoned with their subtle taint... Health, life—
on loan from its opposite, the foreclosure reading:
It's nothing personal; just doing my job.

2. A Citizen Out of Work Explains

Okay, I'm unemployed, and, true, I quit.
My boss can't face his own problems, he needs
A punching bag to bash. I wasn't it.
I'm pounding pavement now, and his heart bleeds—

Not for *that* of course, it's just from missing
The daily rant: How *undesirables*
Are running wild, he caught a pair kissing
In the stairwell! He's sure the stock boy steals!

And you're a moron! Right. So why has he
Started using a megaphone to yell
Down from his office window? It must be
That life without your special moron's hell.

But, hey, abuse just never gave me a buzz.
I'm broke, but so? I have my compensations.
The raw-liver face, the spluttering damnations—
Once only *I* knew. Now everybody does.

3. Olfactory

A wash and wallop nothing had prepared
us for, pushing through automatic doors
(which then closed tight) of the hot subway car.

Ye gods, some passenger hadn't bathed for, what,
a month, a year? Which one? That one, judging
from his once-white face and homeless hair.

Yes, me, he let us know, benign, all smiles,
regal, not the least embarrassed people
fled to the car's far end and cleaved him alone.

A matron frowning in pain, handkerchief
clenched to her face. A blue-jeaned teenager
and girlfriend snickering *gross*'s at the joke.

Keep breathing, it isn't lethal. Next stop
brought in fresh shock troops of battered shoppers,
some pirouetting to skip out, and others

frightened, but staying, intimate with millions
of molecules diffused into the air,
his body's vehement incivility.

The power of smell. Here's poverty and death
and putrefaction you'll break stones, move mountains
to get away from, inferno as a stench.

But think how pure elation comes by the same
sense—as it did once on a South Seas island,
a strip of black sand, plumeria in bloom…

Love, if the gods forgot, might have invented
those flowers' lush, hypnotic say, spice grains
of fragrance infiltrating the seaspray

sent aloft as waves stumbled on relics
of geologic insurrection. Eerie
how, after abrupt cones of lava rose

from oceanic oozes and froze to a halt,
adamant wind and waves abraded, pounded,
plant-kingdom passengers sprang up on board,

a crater gentled into sand, grease-black,
shivering with stars of silica—the beach
at noon so hot it takes your breath away.

4. Hudson Heights

The twain do sometimes meet, desert light
and dryness a brilliant match for this year's rainless fall,
gold leaves cycling down from their hardwoods,
while one last catbird gears up for the crisp flight south.

The married woman strolling among reckless
yellow pinwheels still finds in them a surprise equal
to the first a northeastern autumn sprang
on someone who, as a girl, had run and screamed
through sprinklers on a lawn in La Jolla.

Labor Day, her youngest packed and left
for school, in his wake, the famous "empty-nest
syndrome." Which helps explain tingling magnetic fields
that lately center around Joaquín of Hudson Hardware—
his nostalgic Spanish voice, his eyes' respectful guesswork.

A visit from her twin, high on a Mexican divorce,
salved, but solved exactly nothing.

Far down, steeply down, the train tracks' trellis, which
a delayed express will soon be climbing. And here
in the park, twining, red-leafed Virginia creeper
has borrowed an oak to give it a leg up in the world.
How deep in the earth would tree roots have to dig
to touch the coal that locomotives used to burn?

Low thrums, a rumble, a rush, and there it is:
Train, take me with you, please, north, south, east,
west, anywhere, I don't care, I've stayed slender,
my eyes still sparkle, they have that uncommon color
halfway between blue and green.

5. Who Said That?

The loose-furled, sopping black umbrella
lets its silver spike dribble mercury
beads of cold rain in a ragged line
along the hall carpet his boots track mud on…

Through the window, ARTESIA's single
water tower standing on the outskirts
like a tall barstool, the focal point
for a clump of benumbed oil pumps
that haven't pumped a drop since '89.

Drunk. And has been for years,
hankering away his daydreams, listening
for what exactly. At times your ear
comes near to hearing the sweetheart deal
it wants to hear through a tear
in the rain-soaked realm of debt and fear
of deeper debt, frustrated, ne'er-do-well
afternoons and twilights drowned in malt beer.

Clouds part, the sky sends its sober,
red-and-gold valentine to the Missouri
Ozarks. Black capitals on their stolid tower
confirm the obscure destination.

She does remember. And thought of you last night.

The American Hop Hornbeam

Ostrya virginiana

The tree we have instead of Europe's linden,
tough as horn, hence also known as ironwood—
hewn by yester adzes into axe-hafts,
by yeomen into beams to yoke their ox-teams,
and builders to fit your belfry with a bell.

The genus named by Pliny *Ostrya* a more
exact taxonomy would term a birch,
the New World type (like dozens not its kin)
garnering a surname with a creole ring to it.

An understory tree, preferring gravelly,
xeric soil, the dense, green shade of woodland
giants won't stunt this latecomer's forty leafy feet
nor winter ice break off its tempered branches.
Gray or reddish-brown, deep-grooved in strips,
with laminae that curl and peel, the bark's
knack is to spiral up a trunk to limbs
where catkins hang till spring warmth stirs them,
the male dusters extending some two inches long,
the female flowers modestly low-profile.

From which in summer come small seed-holding husks,
flat nutlets wrapped in a thin sac all over
velveted with fine, stiff hairs, and several
packets to a stem. Their chipper resemblance
to hop fruit explains part of the popular name,
strength (said twice to make sure) the "horn."

And "beam"? Indo-European antecedents,
pre-Pliny by millennia, backtrack to a central
taproot *bheu-*: "to exist," "to grow," evolving,
as it fed the wordtree's trunk and offshoots,
into Latin *fieri,* "to become," and, in the druid
north, a seed for *beon,* Old English's "to be."

From that same forebear we get *beam,* "tree,"
a stanchion for houses or ships; meet figure also
for stalwart shafts of light, like those bright "horns"
the Vulgate said broke forth from Moses' forehead
when he came down from Sinai and the great I AM.

One Cenozoic outcome of the fiats in Genesis
is this limber, sinewed North American indigene,
the sapwood blond, the duramen (or heartwood) mocha,
slow-growing, thus better planted early than late.
Your lot already has one? Then you can settle beneath it,
spine propped, and read: *Because the hornbeam fights*
off rot, cross sections of its cut-down seniors
are oftentimes laid under contribution
by dendrochronology, which finds some hundred
years targeted in the xylograph's ample or lean
response to whatever rains or drought a seedling
first enjoyed (or sapling suffered) in the beginning—
O spark of being dropped into still waters, concentric
echoes swelling, ringing the changes, in rings and rings and rings...

Audubon's Green-Shank*

Glottis nebularia

Sighted, his records claim, on Sand Key, an Old World
species not before or since noted in North America,
thus relegated to the Hypotheticals.

Still, a creditable, forward-leaning shoreline bird,
needle beak all the better to skewer a crablet with
(silhouette much like those aviform scissors I once had),
the name-conferring stalklike legs gray-green,
each constructed with, no, not a knee, a backwards-bending
elbow, a scaly shin, and four talons,
one vestigial.

Audubon the fictionist
monumentalized his subject in St. Augustine,
the gray Castillo de San Marcos in the background,
its turret matching the subject of a snapshot
developed and redeveloped in memory's solutions
since my first visit there, July of 1949.
That image floats and wavers in the neutral bay
printed a century plus before I peeped from the ramparts
of a fort even in the 1830s
as much a displaced person as the green-shank—
Hispanic relic in a territory
that wouldn't for another decade be admitted to the Union.

At a distance, houses of the town, among them
the unpalatial, tabby-walled retreat of Achille Murat,
an exile Emerson had met, on his voyage south, and praised
as a fine specimen of freethinking Empire nobility.

This poem is not meant as an allegory.

The shorebird's brain wasn't designed for such concerns;
but for the drift of weather, or a clouded sunset, yes...
A devotee of Nature troubled even so to paint this village,
its fortress and cannon, site a dreamy kid would later absorb
before he (I mean I) knew what to make of it, on the brink
of hatching into some bird or other of America—
but not into a green-shank, no, no, not the green-shank.

To a Jack-in-the-Box

Allowed your fondest druthers, *you'd* stay put.
But, no, to prove a point, they'll pop your hood,
Cut the slinky coil you've banked some slack,
Describe Old Faithful's spritz as resurrection.

Tethered effigy with never a foot
(A defect your cap and bells don't quite make good),
You'll be acclaimed for buoyancies you lack,
As though clique-claque could boost a toy's dejection.

Oh, not that you don't smile: in paint, you do.
How often pranks and cracks paid off the gloom!
Yet, when the real thing came too close, you fled,

Clapped shut (and sealed) the lid of Xanadu.
Your clan, with traces of their former bloom,
Now gather to unbury their undead.

Deinos

In Attic Greek, "clever," but, also, "dire."
Makes sense: When wit and nuance hone their edge,
the cleaver keen enough to split a hair
likewise bisects one's skull into hemispheres
neat as a melon's, the lucent flesh of knowledge
laid open for plunder. And small wonder
we vacillate between two puzzled minds
as understanding luffs into the wind,
through the colossal yes and no they hedge.

British intelligence styled their first computer
"Colossus," which tossed the Allies brighter odds
on D-Day, once it cracked the Nazi ENIGMA.
Rough magic masterminded by Alan Turing,
who had wit to burn, a pink-tinged laughing gas
the socially attuned straight off deciphered
as blithe allusions to his tastes. "Too clever
by half," yes, and when criminal and social codes
stood counter to the cleavages he preferred?
No: Half was enough, he'd give apocalypse
free rein, outstrip the green world and its stigma.

A cellar in Plath's New, a kitchen in
Hughes' older England, housed her intended death.
One botched; and then a cleverly hatched putsch
expatriating language from mere flesh—
just as apprenticeship drew a deep breath
and yielded to a *Meister* from the German,
to strong encryptions delved and trafficked in.
An art done well? The dyer's hand subdued
by racing echoes, the pour of aerial blue.

Deinos. Godlike hardship hewn from a marble
frieze, the horses' perfected heads with one
intelligence turning toward eternity,
for golden-haired Sylvia, twice out of nature,
and ashen-haired Alan, on fire with keen
algorithms, dire triangulations of the code.

The Wife to Potiphar

Regret his imprisonment? Yes! I wanted him dead.
But a month or two of Egyptian penal correction
Should serve the purpose. No, I don't miss him, not now.
That's my point, we never—he balked, he wouldn't.
Oh, I liked him at first. Handsome, with *such* eyes... *[Sighs]*

And, like most members of his race, intelligent.
Although, naive. A certain roughness, a crude strength,
Is one way to put it. But a year or so in Egypt
Pumices most of our immigrants to a higher finish.
Hints from myself served as a last, elegant chamois. *[Chuckles]*
Didn't he gauge the effect of those bows, that proffered arm?
Oh, don't worry, he enjoyed our chats. A member of the male
Species dancing attendance on me: I wasn't used
To that. From my husband least of all. A woman in the Nile
Valley? She's a despot's bitch, on whom he sires his whelps.
Potiphar got five—not that he thanked me for a single one.
Children, you see, redress the constraints we labor under.
To lift my spirits, friends always apply the same poultice:
"Your *son* will have the prerogatives you were denied."
Fine. But who ever mistakes the tinny tone of an alibi?
They want to stanch the whining and defuse their own guilt. *[Yawns]*
So tiresome, curled up in your bedding like a ripe melon,
Gazing at the frieze opposite, in the vain hope mere
Figments will draw you into their blue-and-green legend.

He saw it all, the frustration, the gloom, as he stood
At my side, consoling me with an ostrich-feather fan.
And with stories apropos his little northern province—
Canaan, what a curious name. One day he said, "Now,
Lady, isn't it time you put yourself first?" And that,
That could mean only one thing. One lovely thing.

Or so I imagined. He led me a merry dance, the rascal.
Here's your new adventure: pursuing a virginal youth! *[Laughs out loud]*
At one point we were racing around the garden shrubs.
And having exhausted other defenses, the poor booby
Feigned his tastes went in *another direction.* Am I a fool,
Have I never been at court, never seen that sort swanning
About, flinging themselves on each other's necks? *[Grunts]*
Joseph was made of a different clay. The strong grip, the warmth.
Looking into his eyes, you saw a man, and... depths.
His touch-me-not pose made a pitiful match with all the...
The rest. Am I so homely as to be spurned by a slave?
Giving him a slap was poor strategy, granted. Think
Of my Bubastis when she's after her bird: A cat never leaps,
No, she creeps, creeps, creeps. *Then* pounces. Then brings the limp
Little corpse and drops it on your pillow. Alas, from that day on
My dear, sweet footman no longer trusted me. Truth to tell,
I began to be afraid. What if he blabbed? Well then, one; last; effort.
Those born in the great Sphinx's shadow always, always
Devise contingency plans. Always. Omenoset procured
Some goat's blood, a cup of which we concealed near the bed.
(Now, don't worry, she knows her place, the secret's safe.)

Gently summoned, Joseph came. My robe lay open. And? He shut his eyes!
I took his hand. Warm, callused. But, no, he—*he*—tugged free.
The gall. Thus provoked, who would *not* have screamed, *not* have
Struck at him? He fled, leaving a sash behind. I took the cup and
Poured its contents on... my person. Dashed the clay to pieces
Against the blue tiles there. And went on screaming, screaming
My screams, whipping myself into an ecstasy of rage...

After all, it's one of the few complaints they will take
Seriously. As, in fact, this time, too. My husband did. Joseph
Was dragged away. Did I care? No. No. No. *[Whispers]* No.

So he's gone, and that's that. Meanwhile—aha!—he's been
Replaced. Egypt will never, never lack for slaves, some few
Of them truly devoted. You darling! Mmm. Climb up here.
Bubastis wants a kiss, yes, she does, yes she *does*... You heard what?
Ah, he's doing that now? No one was ever more industrious. Imagine:

Hanging out a shingle—behind bars!—as an interpreter of dreams.

Phantasmachia

One of them sidles up across the bare
ground, brandishing a scrap of oiled red silk,
a mask he swears I've always tried to wear—
and must wear now. What tactic but to block
the scuffle with my fist and forearm? Still,
feinting, jabbing, he manages to stick
it to the temple on one side. And while
I peeled it off, a figure I half recognize
runs up with another—papier-mâché,
cold, gluey—which she plasters to my face.

Stripping both their decals, there! at least
I freed my eyes—as if I wanted to see
crowd hysteria in action, unleashed
gangs that rush forward, rabid to have their way
with the target tackled off his feet and crushed
under their weight, their frenzy for a piece
of the suffocation… You know, just as when
some marine creature has leaked a drop of blood,
sharks home in like torpedoes and begin
to slash and savage, sawteeth ripping flesh
until they've shredded and then junked their scapefish.

No stimulant, no magic, like an image—
which funneled under me a breaker of rage
to throw them off, stand up, and ride the crest
with, "Go ahead, then, lie, turn into stone!
Those projected masks, whose are they? Your own,
possessions blind and feral enough to suggest
packed-down guilt and panic. And the result?
What was a game has now become compulsion,
you can't control it, and so deserve compassion.
But I won't be scratched out by a proxy death."

Attentive hush. The masks drop to the ground.
Assailants, one by one, withdraw... But then
a thick, slump-shouldered figure spins around
and says, "Why should we let him get off free?"

The man who lacks a sense of shame's no man,
I thought. *Choose what you next say carefully.*
Those words will be conveyed on your last breath.

After Ghalib

What artifact has ever brought suit against its Maker?
A picture dressing up in writs gets executed.

Don't ask what wells those melancholy loners drill
To flood the desert with milk and make a dawn of nightfall.

Restraint undone by piercing desire—now *that's* worth seeing,
The blade bereft of its edge as breath forsakes the body.

Reason, set your watchful traps wherever you like.
My theme, my phoenix, soars on gusts the speaker exhales.

Say that I'm bound in chains, flames licking at my feet:
Each link is forged of hair, consumed (as I am!) in fire.

Whether

Whether anger quickens a lagging stride,
and periodic burn-offs in the forest
revitalize exhausted soil and flora—.
Whether we should take pleasure in the wildcat

jubilation of a lightning bolt
that whips its silver vein of genesis
through the night sky, flash-photo of a white
birch upended, the root-system buckled

to swollen thunderheads—. And whether naming
an offense amounts to sour grapes and common
bitterness, or even the conceited nonsense
of unwashed yahoo multitudes, a yawping

insult to civilized behavior—. Whether
a July rainstorm, even when it drenches
the unprepared pedestrian and befuddles
traffic, might be extravagant, a joy,

like the whoops and escalating bop glissandos
of Gillespie's upraised horn, cascading pitches
a countersong to meteoric chalk marks
Perseids burn across the House of Leo—.

And whether peaceful ecstasy might float
up from a fifteen-second avalanche
reflected in the skier's goggles, his jacket
a spark of scarlet on the topmost slope,

waiting for the homeward track to clear.

New York Three Decades On

Jazz cuts through narrative nostalgia—
Louis Armstrong reinventing Storyville
on someone's chrome transistor up the platform
that late August I stepped off the train.
125th Street, East Side—which looked,
on the map, like an easy half-mile to Columbia,
I mean, as the crow flies. I wasn't flying, though,
and here it was: Harlem 1965-style,
still in mourning for Malcolm X,
strung out, almost crazy with America.
Even in that frame-up, people had errands,
in and out of the storefronts, driving off
in gleaming Imperials and battered Mustangs.
Essence on the newsstands, call-and-response
of Haitian and Alabama voices;
but nobody challenged me, no flat-broke
brothers hustled this out-of-it honky,
it just now dawning on him where he was.

I was in New York, where I'd wanted to be,
an existential French Lit grad student
in Morningside Heights, agog, strolling through
those first unfettered weeks, with every radio
in Fun City blaring Phil Spector's *wall of sound...*
My rented room's ancient, scumbled plaster
mimicked the meteoric surface of the moon.
So I tacked up a green bedspread and, to that,
Lautrec's *Aristide Bruant dans son cabaret.*
A neat match for the 1890s
Art Nouveau walnut headboard of the bed
and my landlady's marble-topped dresser,
its fogged mirror tilting forward and down,
a pensive cockroach scoping out the frame...
Free at last in *La Bohème.*

Gotham City wasn't gratis, though.
Even those grubby digs cost (back then not peanuts,
or not to me) ten bucks a week. So just skip lunch
and, at afternoon tea in Philosophy Hall,
scarf down Oreo after Oreo—sweet dominoes
fanned in a half-circle on gold-rimmed china.
Outside the window, a huge bronze *Thinker,*
whose pose I assumed every morning,
staring at the crackled gray enamel of a bathtub
Mrs. Smith was too blind and feeble to scour,
oppressed by the *existential void...*
This was how to weigh imponderables, and where
should the singer of inexperience go?—clueless,
friendless, always on the lookout for Mr. Right,
a face without features, imagination's starbright X.

Was that you at the seminar table commenting
on doubt in Montaigne to Professor Frame?
You in the lobby of the New York State Theater
cruising the intermission between *Apollo*
and *Western Symphony*? You, slouching
into the Thalia for a matinee of *Breathless*?

I went to JULIUS', slid onto a barstool
and scanned the silvery quadrant that, across
a phalanx of spouted bottles, returned my stare.
Desperate, lonely—where better take that rap
than Metropolis, its solitary angst
the foundation of an urban cult with scriptures
by Baudelaire and Whitman, Rimbaud, the Beats.
My turtleneck, espresso black, dressed the part—
my unfiltered Gauloises and buckled Wellingtons:
For the first time, by being a misfit, I fit in.

Day long, and into midnight, during the subway strike,
avenues choked on traffic and exhaust. Strikers won,
and the two-bits fare went the way of Penn Station.
On the night of the Great Blackout, I skipped town
to Jersey with a (distant) marriage prospect
who was bunking at a friend's in East Orange.
We'd connected last May back home—so tell me, Cupid,
can passion be rekindled in a single night?
The Blackout party I missed, but not the fun.
Mr. Right in every way but one: He didn't live in New York.

Next day, returning, the bus slowed and coasted
toward Lincoln Tunnel. Fading trace of last night's tryst,
the grin on my face also registered a city-mouse thrill
that the backlit horizon of highrise Manhattan
looked like home. It *was* home, and I on my way there,
Aristide astride his new citizenship, habitué
of dark cafés, an existence that preceded
essence, stills from my movie, frame after frame,
smoking philosophy along with Bird
and Miles, starring a sentence in the Selected
Rimbaud: "Love must be reinvented."

Replacing a Part

Why be startled if the grease monkeys
working on my hatchback are Asian,
considering this mishap befell on the fringes
of Chinatown? Not me but others were treated
to a scream of sparks as the exhaust pipe
dragged along Canal, an unscheduled act
in the nighttime light-show of neon,
traffic signals, and, above all, the moon,
afloat in a scattering of stars.

Repairs so minor take only minutes,
and this one comes with a view. Good-looking
in their jumpsuits, fleet, they wield their tools
with flashy nonchalance, scooting under and out
the hoist frame, obligatory smears of lube
on hands and face. Which only makes them more
appealing, as the one whose zipper has plunged
almost to the navel seems to know. Our eyes meet,
but—nothing more. In the universal beauty
competition, some contestants like to
tease, collecting votes, and gender no object.
The gravitational attraction of sublunar
bodies would weigh less with me
if I weren't newly single; but I am. I am.
The labor, the exhaustion in that word.

Set your sights on higher things. Up there,
the Temple of Heaven, cosmology's suspended
monitor that fabulists once animated
with beasts and heroes by connecting
a thousand stellar dots. Spring Moon, tonight's
Miss Universe, spotlit by offstage solar power,

slides across the darkness, stars and stars
in her wake... A minute hand for imagination's
oldest and vastest clock, the one that always leads
to speculation re the clockmaker.

Why should there have ever been anything
rather than nothing? Head-on collision
with that question leaves thought totaled.
Instead, it tabulates the facts of motion,
number, scheduling the nadir
or the zenith of the sundial,
how many years it takes a beam of starlight
to drive to Planet Earth—
celestial mechanics infinitely more
earthshaking than our homegrown zodiac.

Now, human reckoning has projected us
into a third thousand, where new years will keep on
moving as they did before—I mean, if time continues
as a conscious fact. Will it heal all things
by the arrival of the fourth? For that matter,
why should we ever have had time at all?
I guess because Being got tired of being nothing.
It was lonely, it wanted to become someone
able to love and to cease not loving.

Overture

The warblers' startling *alba* at five am
through white and green square miles of pine and birch—
a benchmark in the woodland record exceeded
as the sun mounts a steep blue flight of stairs.

*

Gazes sometimes lock and linger ages longer
than regulation, no appeal so fateful
as a mild question couched in dark but shining eyes.
before: a hand going out to rest lightly
on parted lips; and a sigh breathes its lifelong after.

*

"Proceed as way opens," say the Quakers, and way
with you is like being one with them, this trembling
and protected meeting, an Inside Passage read
by touch (spelunkers in prehistory),
the juncture that spirit strikes, almighty, twice.

*

Passion, reflection, speech, and action once covert,
spill from the spout, a boost to spring seedlings.
Fresh-kindled rapids have rinsed away this morning's sweat,
their twined, downplunging coolant a spangled gown
for Isadora freely espousing *Egmont, Fidelio,*
sequence on sequence of splashing eighth-notes (CRASH)
and a cymbal of fire meets its double in the rippled pool.

To a Lover Who Is HIV-Positive

You ask what I feel.
Grief; and a hope
that springs from your intention
to forward projects as assertive
or lasting as flesh ever upholds.

Love; and a fear
that the so far implacable
cunning of a virus will smuggle away
substantial warmth, the face, the response
telling us who we are and might be.

Guilt; and bewilderment
that, through no special virtue of mine
or fault of yours, a shadowed affliction
overlooked me and settled on you. As if
all, always, got what was theirs.

Anger; and knowledge
that our venture won't be joined
in perfect safety. Still, it's better odds
than the risk of not feeling much at all.
Until you see yourself well in them,
love, keep looking in my eyes.

Coltrane's "Equinox"

Quartet, with Trane's tenor, McCoy Tyner on piano.
Mainly their duo, plus Elvin Jones' punctual,
downplayed drums, the thumbed bass from Steve Davis.
But the bare facts don't explain what happened

that October of 1960 when prophecy
roundhoused the sound studio. Then and now
drum and piano strike up a Latino intro,
so you know you're there in the *Barrio,*

after which, the tenor's casual entrance,
a little foxtrot forward, back, forward,
the tune no more than twenty get-lost bars
mostly in minor thirds, discontent, smoldering

like some rusty oil drum in a vacant lot
on 133rd Street, the improvised trashbin
somebody came along and fired up, hell,
just to watch a nylon of smoke rise above it all.

For your basic despair, blues chords will do,
yet, if Trane by moments lifts off into a jagged
flight, he still owns the shape of his skipstep
theme, which knocks one same note eight times

to say, "This is over, over, over." Then Tyner
steps into his solo—a cold trance in stainless-steel
octaves that repeat more often than they shift,
high up, strolling across a rooftop, looking out

over the available real estate, the morning-after
cityscape you'll never split from, if you were
born here, understand? *Not in our lifetime*
the man's not going to quit that white horse

going to run the whole race not enough of us will
get out the way it all comes down to are you bitter
no that's not the word blue yes but when when we
when we play that whatever got lost we own

Seeing All the Vermeers

Met Museum, 1965, the first
I'll see, his *Young Woman Sleeping.*
Stage right, bright-threaded carpet flung over the table
where a plate of apples, crumpled napkin
and drained wineglass abut the recapped pitcher.
Propped by one hand, her leaning drowse,
behind which, a door opens on the dream, dim, bare
but for a console and framed mirror—or a painting
too shadowed to make out. Next to it,
(certitude) one window, shuttered for the duration....

That dream also timed *me* out, a lull in the boomeranging
hubbub of the staggering city I'd just moved to.

*

In the Frick's *Officer and Laughing Girl,* spring sunshine
entered left, partly blocked by the noncom suitor's hat-brim,
wide, dark as seduction, conquest. A map dotted with schooners
backed her fresh elations, the glass winking at them both.... He'd see
why, in a later day, crewcut recruits were shipping out to Nam;
and she, why the student left was up in arms against the war.

*

In '67, Ann and I spent a graduate year in Paris;
and lived in the Louvre, too, along with *The Lacemaker*—
self-effacing, monumental, an artisan
whose patience matched the painter's, inscribed
in tangling skeins of scarlet oil against an indigo
silk cushion. Silent excruciation

among toy spools framed the bald paradox
termed "women's work," disgracing anything less
than entire devotion to labor entered into. (That May,
a million demonstrators marched up the Champs Elysées.)

*

From there to Amsterdam and *The Little Street*,
where innate civility distilled a local cordial, free
from upheaval, from dearth *and* opulence, each brick
distinct, their collectivity made credible
by a chalky varicosis that riddled foreground façades.
A century's successive mortars filled those cracks,
nor will the figures down on hands and knees in the foreground
stand up again till they've replaced that broken tile.

The Woman in Blue Reading a Letter calmed misgivings
with the global trust that swelled her body, a soft counterweight
to expeditions tracked across the weathered map behind.
A new-found Eden, festooned with portents, history
piloting ship and cargo across the wrinkling sea.

The *Maidservant Pouring Milk*'s power to see
in threadbare clothes and plain features a meek radiance
made of *caritas,* doesn't need words… But since I do,
call her a velvet motet developed in blue, in scaled-down
yellow-green that I could hear, the resonant stillness
centered on movement's figment, cream paint paying out
a corded rivulet at the cruse's lip. Crusty loaves, nail-holes
in plaster, and knuckles roughened by scalds and scrubs
witnessed to the daily immolation, performed as first light
tolled matins from a dutch-gold vessel hooked to the wall.

*

By train to Den Haag, to see the *View of Delft*'s ink-black
medieval walls and bridge, barges anchored on a satin
water more pensive than the clouded blue above,
where one tall steeple took its accolade of sun.
(Proust's "patch of yellow wall" I couldn't find, though.)

The *Girl in a Turban* looked like Anne Wiazemsky,
Godard's new partner, whom we'd seen in his latest film.
Liquid eyes, half-parted lips, a brushstroke ancillary
to fable highlighting the weighty pearl at her earlobe,
her "Turkish" costume stage-worthy, if she ever chose to act.

*

By then it was set: No matter how many years or flights
it took, I'd see all of Vermeer—which helps explain
the Vienna stop we made that spring, and our instant beeline
to *An Artist in His Studio* (called, today, *The Allegory of Fame*).
What to make of the Artist's bloomers, outmoded even then—

and why would his model hold book and clarion, standing
before the mapped Low Countries? If that anesthetized mask
on the table near her denied the chandelier its candles,
then who hung a tapestried curtain in the left foreground?

Vermeer; but his meaning subverts comment, always
less hypnotic than the surface itself, a luminous
glaze adhering to receding frames in series,
chromatic theaters for featured roles that also kindle
fervor in their supporting actor, the secret soul.

*

Strike me dumb on first seeing *The Astronomer*
in Guy de Rothschild's study—well, a photograph of it
in an '80s coffee-table book, *The Great Houses
of Paris*. Not long after, thanks to philanthropy
and the tax structure, it devolved upon the state.
Semester break that winter, McC. and I jetted to France,
entered the Louvre's new glass pyramid and fought
dense crowds to where he hung, *The Lacemaker*'s late consort.
In a brown studio, his fingers reading the globe,
he sat, immovably dutiful to calculations
devised ad hoc to safecrack the star-studded zodiac.

*

I was one of the visitors tiptoeing
through Isabella Gardner's house in Boston
decades before the heist, which to this day
remains unsolved. But balance one instance
of good luck against a trip made to Ireland
in '86, missing by only a few months
the Beit Collection's *Lady Writing a Letter*.
Paid so often now, the compliment of theft
puts a keen edge on our art pilgrimages:
The icon may be gone when you arrive.

That fall, I lived in London's Camden Town,
writing on… call them stateside topics; and soon
tubed up to Kenwood House, relieved to find
their prime collectible unstolen—its potential
as ecphrastic plunder not apparent at the time.
(A sonnet, no less, completed earlier in New Haven,
qualified me for that satire on the Connecticut bard
besotted with Vermeer. Still, subjects could be barred
in advance only if they and poems were the same gadget.
Disbelief, you're suspended, even for the standard
gloat over shots knocked back at the Cedar Tavern,
ca. 1950, with Pollock and de Kooning.)

Here then was Kenwood's *Lady with Guitar*, in corkscrew
curls, lemon jacket trimmed with ermine, lounging
like some hippie denizen of Washington Square,
strumming for the nth time his secondhand Dylan...
Maybe they heard her, too, the National Gallery's
paired women portraits, each playing a virginal,
both in silk dresses, one seated, one standing—
Profane and Sacred Love, if the old allegory fits.

A trip from London to Edinburgh produced, beyond
the classic-Gothic limestone city grimed with soot,
an early *Christ in the House of Mary and Martha*,
conceived before the painter's parables began unfolding
at home in Delft. Still, Martha's proffered pannier is as real
as the bread it holds, and Jesus' open hand, rendered
against clean table linen, as strong and solid as Vermeer's.

*

A chill, damp March in Dresden with Chris.
We'd begun with the Berlin State Museum's holdings
and then trained down on our way to Prague.
The Gemäldegalerie, quiet as a church, listened
while beads of tarnished rain pelted the skylights.
Works known from reproductions offered themselves
to the gray ambient, visibly conscious
of having survived Allied firebombs fifty years
earlier and a postwar Ice Age that slammed home,
then froze every bolt in the Eastern sector.
Young Vermeer's *The Procuress* makes love for sale
push beyond the sour analogue
of art-as-commerce into distinct portraits,
comedic types you have and haven't seen before
caught up in cheerful barter while wine flows
at a balustrade draped with carpet and a fur cape.
The client's left hand could have been mine,

weighing down a pretty shoulder (and the bodice),
but not the right, poised to let fall a coin
into her open palm. Men's hunger for sex
and poverty's for comforts—an old story,
mean or tragic, and never finally resolved.

*

Having missed Her Majesty's *The Music Lesson*, lent
over the years to several exhibitions, guess who danced
when told that it would grace the show to end all shows
scheduled in Washington, the fall of '95.
And other hard-to-sees from Brunswick and Frankfurt—
jubilation—were included also, plus
apprentice works on pagan or religious themes.
Long caterpillar of a line, composed of hundreds
come to worship art and its obsessive love of life.
An hour's wait on aching legs, and in we go:
The Geographer, taking his place by *The Astronomer*,
Ireland's letter-writer, look, recaptured, and now restored
to the public; a *View of Delft*, cleaned so thoroughly
you couldn't miss that patch of yellow—*not* a wall,
Proust got it wrong, instead, a roof… Sheltering involuntary
memories of countless choked-up viewers,
whose gazes added one more laminate of homage
to a surface charged with how many hundred thousands now.

From the permanent collection—why?—I saw as though
I never had the *Woman Weighing Gold*, some twenty years
(gone, and still here) since that first visit (Walter with me)
to the National Gallery. By word-origin *Galilees*,
international through their holdings, these cathedrals
of art draw in the faithful that faith in art has summoned
for mutual appraisal, what we are seen in what we see.

Hence the scales at center canvas Vermeer suspended
from her fine-boned hand, the face all understanding
and, so, forgiving all. Nevertheless, the great maternal
judge weighs one gold (a ring? a coin?) against a smaller gold,
in gloom as dark as the Day of Wrath, whose millennial
trumpet tears away a final veil.
                              So human error
will yield, her calm demeanor says, to *Pax caelestis*
and dawn break forth in perpetual light transforming
breath, strife, treasure, theft, love, and the end of love,
into its own substance—strong, bright beam of Libra rising
step by step up the scale to Eden and a countenance
the soul, made visible, is now accorded grace to see.

Around us, heads bent toward a morning vintaged
more than three hundred years ago. Manifold delight
wearing Nikes, Levi's, parkas; students, grizzled veterans,
young mothers, teachers, painters—awestruck, whispering
Heavens! Just look at that!—his New World public.

Acknowledgments

Some of the work that went into this volume was done during residencies at Yaddo in 1998 and 2001, and at the Château de Lavigny in 2000. Thanks are due to the Corporation of Yaddo and to the Ledig-Rowohlt Foundation.

I would like to thank the editors of the following magazines where poems in this volume first appeared, sometimes in different form:

American Poetry Review, "Intervals" and "And Then I Saw"
The Anglican Theological Review, "Jerusalem" (first version)
Anthropophagy, "A Citizen Out of Work Explains" and "Overture"
The Appalachee Review, "Olfactory"
Barrow Street, "Bloodwork"
Beloit Poetry Journal, "The Bandwagon," "Solstice" (now "Memory"), and "After Celan"
Black Book, "Whether"
Boston Review, "The Report of My Death Was an Exaggeration"
Carlton Poetry Review, "A Window on the Strait of Juan de Fuca"
Columbia, "Coltrane's 'Equinox'" and "To a Lover Who Is HIV-Positive"
The Drunken Boat, "After Ghalib"
Gadfly, "Dawn of Evening"
Image, "Jerusalem" (second version)
The James White Review, "Double Portrait with Refrigerator Magnets," "My Last June in Chelsea," "Long-Distance Call to a Friend Who Lived with AIDS As Long As He Could," and "Phantasmachia"
Leviathan, "Jerusalem" (reprinted second version)
The Nation, "The Common Thread"
New England Review, "Hudson Heights"
The Oxford American, "Who Said That?"
Paris Review, "Who, What, Where, When, Why?," "To a Jack-in-the-Box," and "The Wife to Potiphar"
PN Review, "The Common Thread" and "Tenebrae"
Poetry, "Audubon's Green-Shank" and "Seeing All the Vermeers"
The Princeton Library Chronicle, "Deinos"
Raritan Quarterly, "Tenebrae" and "New York Three Decades On"

Slate, "Asynchronic" and "Photography"
Theology Today, "The Author of Torah"
Verse, "A Walrus Tusk from Alaska"
Western Humanities Review, "The American Hop Hornbeam" and
  "The Mousetrap"

"And Then I Saw" was reprinted in *Blood and Tears: Poems for Matthew Shepard.* "A Walrus Tusk from Alaska" was reprinted in *The New Bread Loaf Anthology of Contemporary American Poetry,* Michael Collier and Stanley Plumly, editors; and in *The Making of a Poem,* Eavan Boland and Mark Strand, editors.

About the Author

Alfred Corn is the author of eight earlier books of poetry, a novel, a study of prosody, and a collection of essays. A recipient of fellowships from the Guggenheim Foundation, the Academy of American Poets, and the NEA, among others, Corn has traveled widely, but has made New York City his primary residence. As an art critic, he writes for *Art in America* and *ARTNews*; his poems appear regularly in *The Nation*, *The Paris Review*, and *Slate*. He has taught at Yale, UCLA, Columbia University, and for 2001–2002 held the Bell Chair at the University of Tulsa.

The Chinese character for poetry is made up of two parts: "word" and "temple."
It also serves as pressmark for Copper Canyon Press.

Founded in 1972, Copper Canyon Press remains dedicated to publishing poetry
exclusively, from Nobel laureates to new and emerging authors. The Press
thrives with the generous patronage of readers, writers, booksellers, librarians,
teachers, students, and funders—everyone who shares the conviction that poetry
invigorates the language and sharpens our appreciation of the world.

PUBLISHERS' CIRCLE
The Allen Foundation for the Arts
The Breneman Jaech Foundation
Lannan Foundation
National Endowment for the Arts

EDITORS' CIRCLE
Thatcher Bailey
Cynthia Hartwig and Tom Booster
Port Townsend Paper Company
Target Stores
Emily Warn and Daj Oberg
Washington State Arts Commission

FOR INFORMATION AND CATALOGS:
COPPER CANYON PRESS
Post Office Box 271
Port Townsend, Washington 98368
360/385-4925
www.coppercanyonpress.org